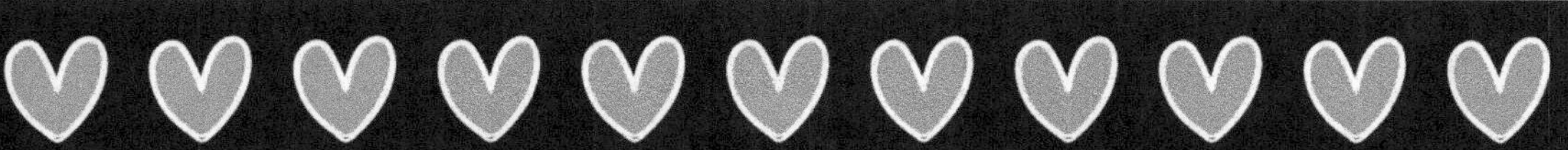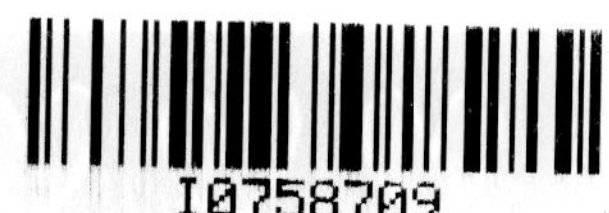

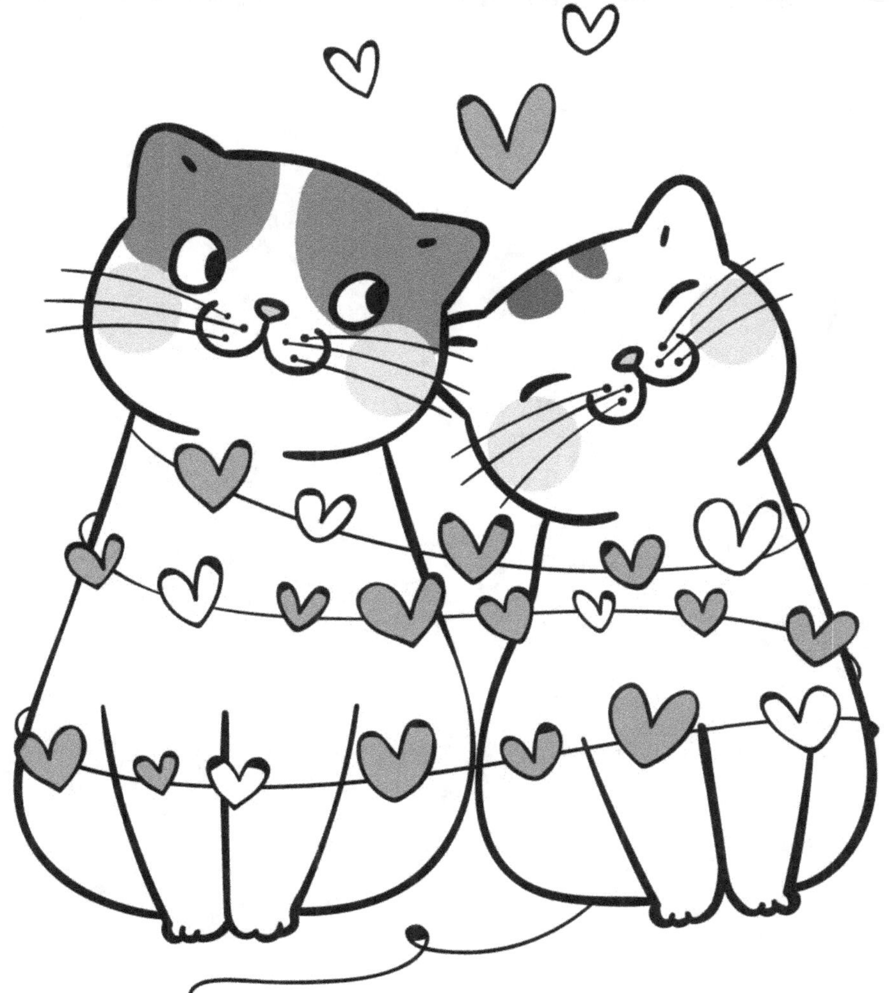

THIS BOOK BELONG TO ....

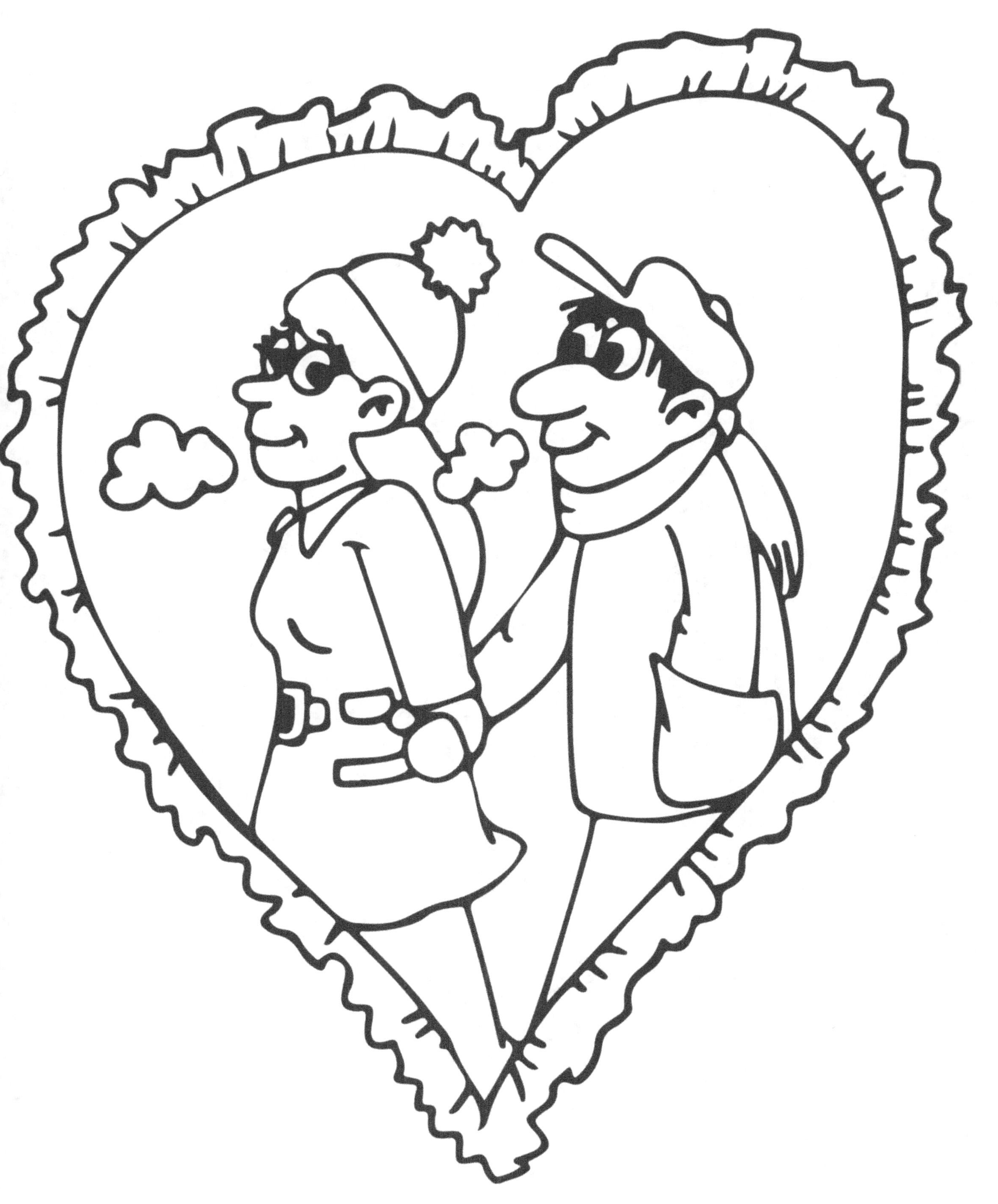

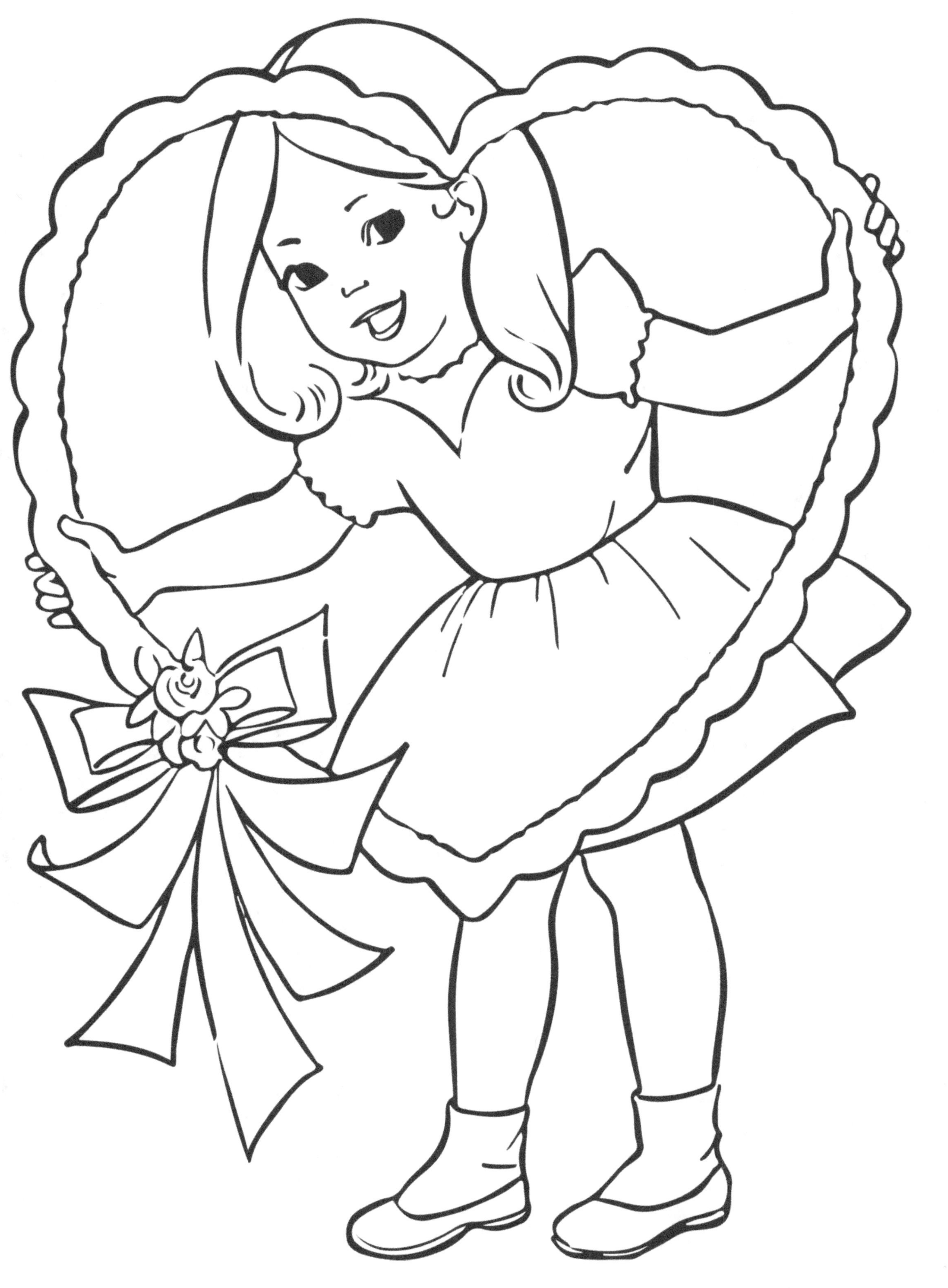

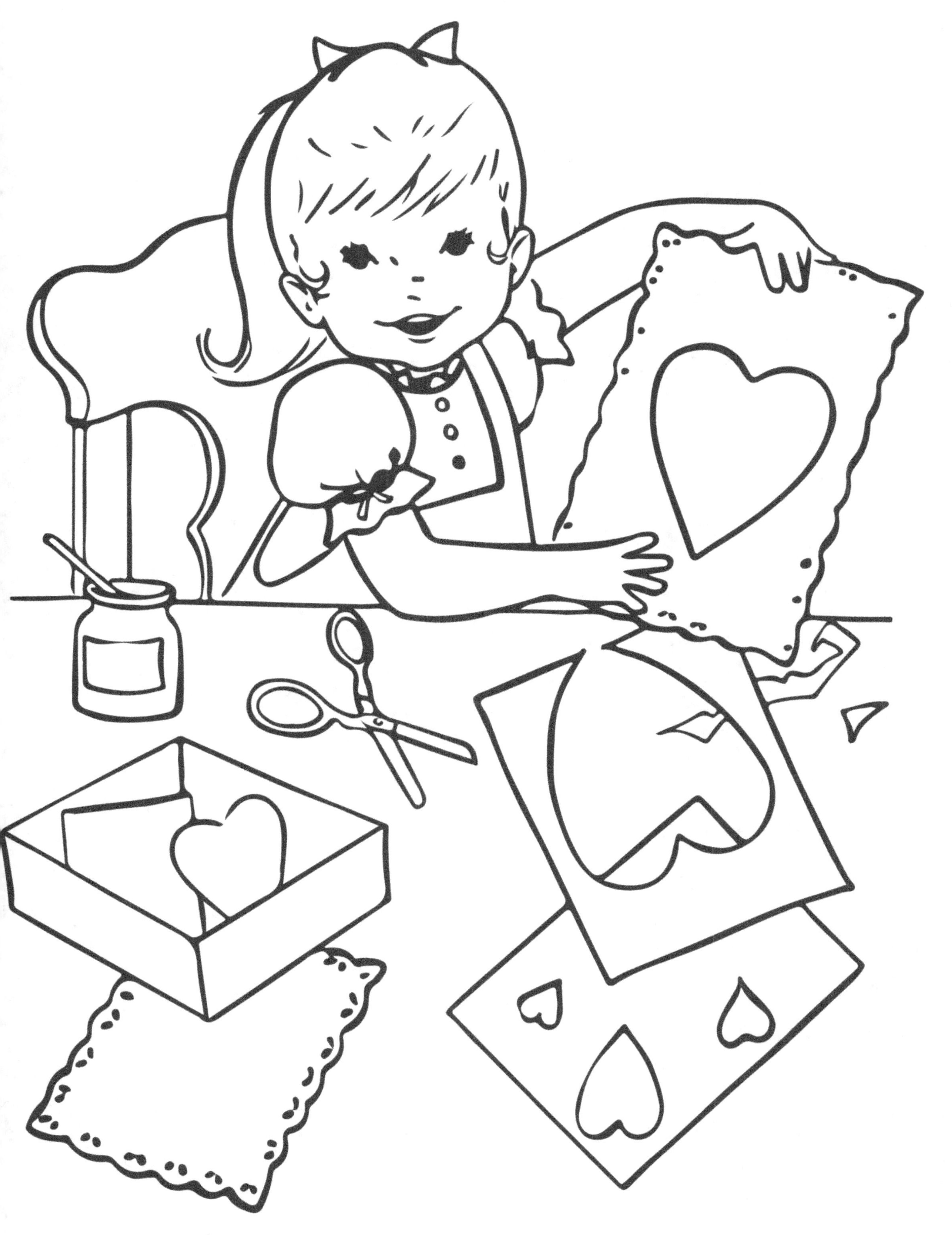

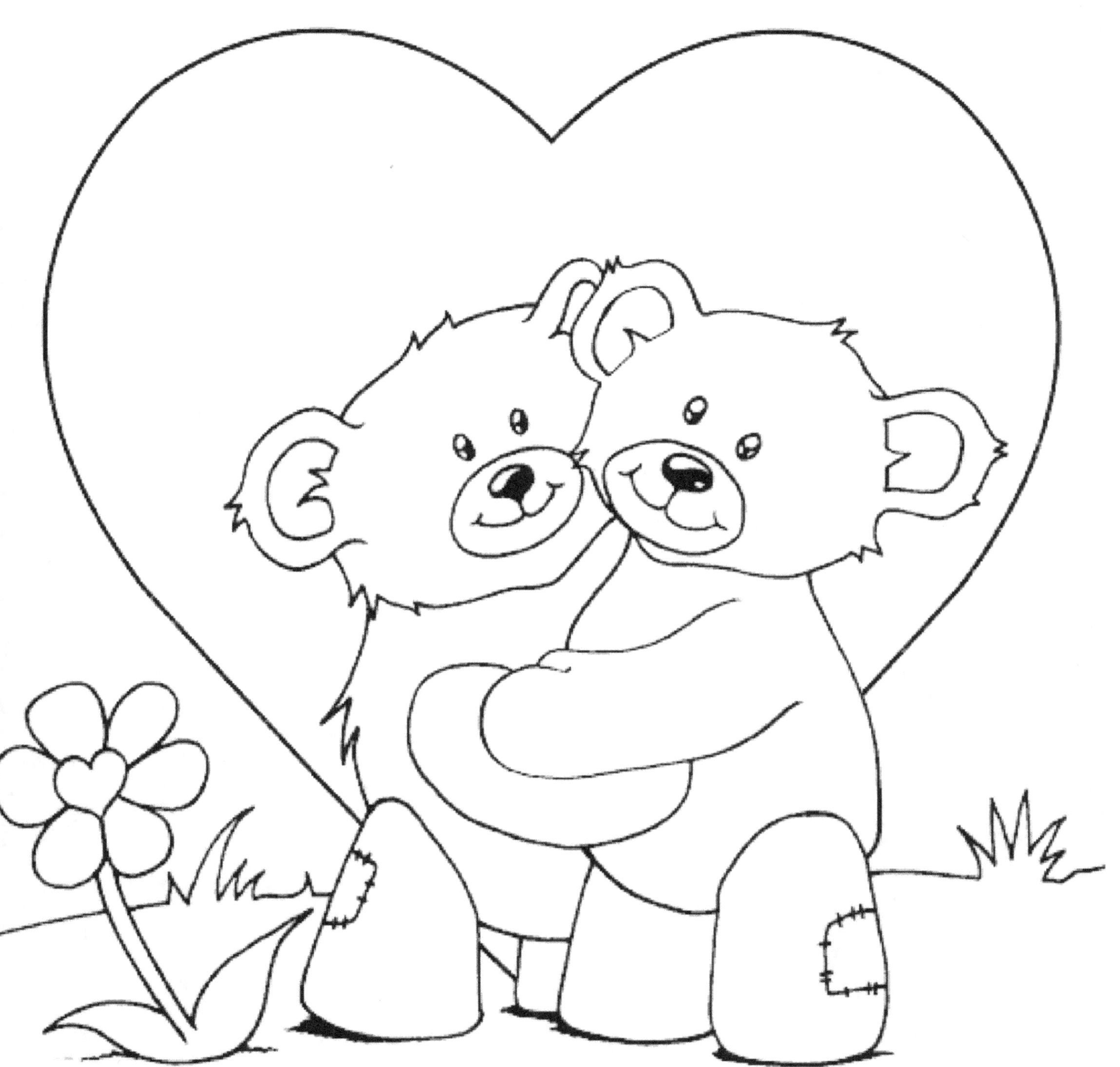

Happy Valentine's Day

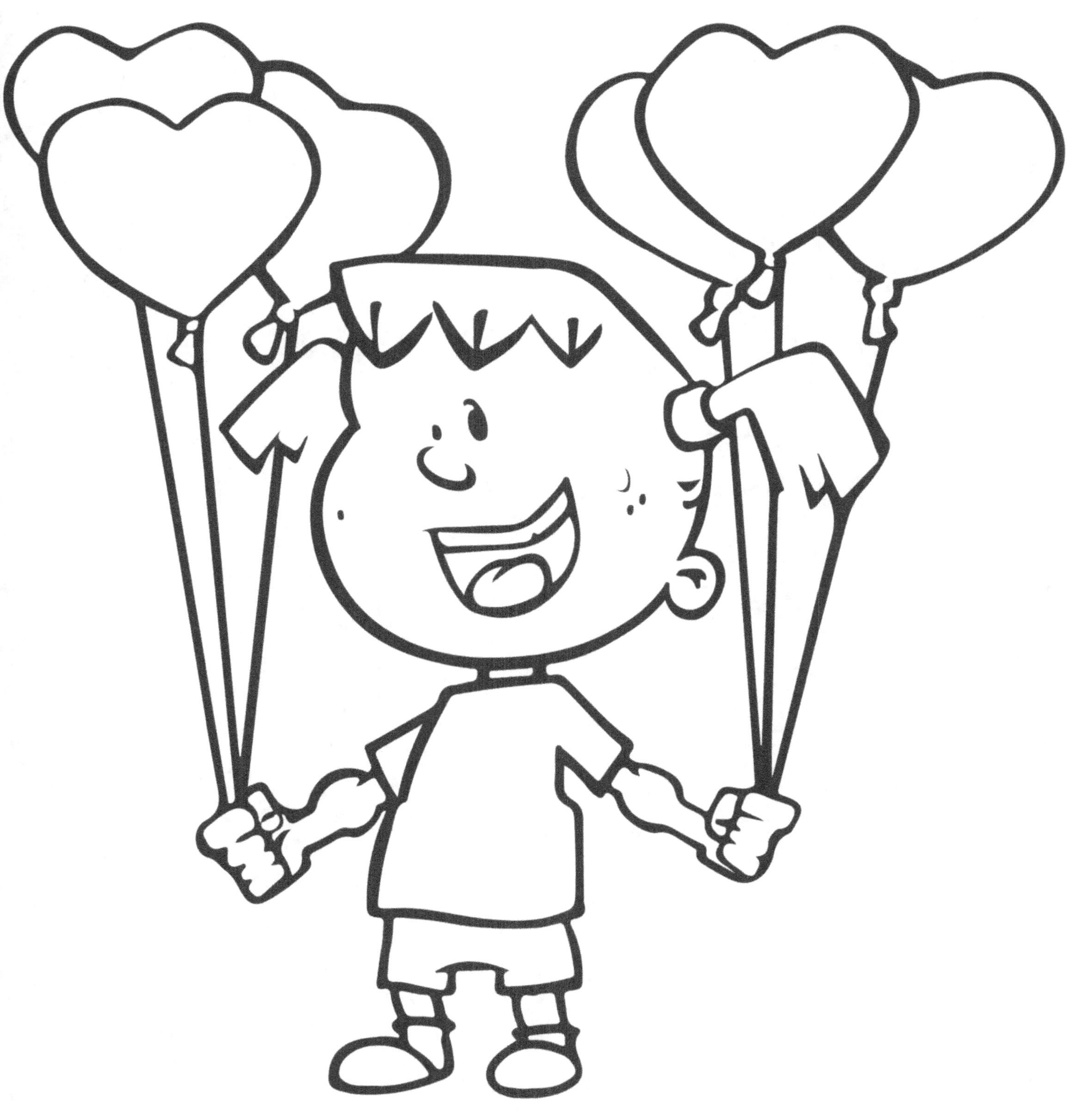

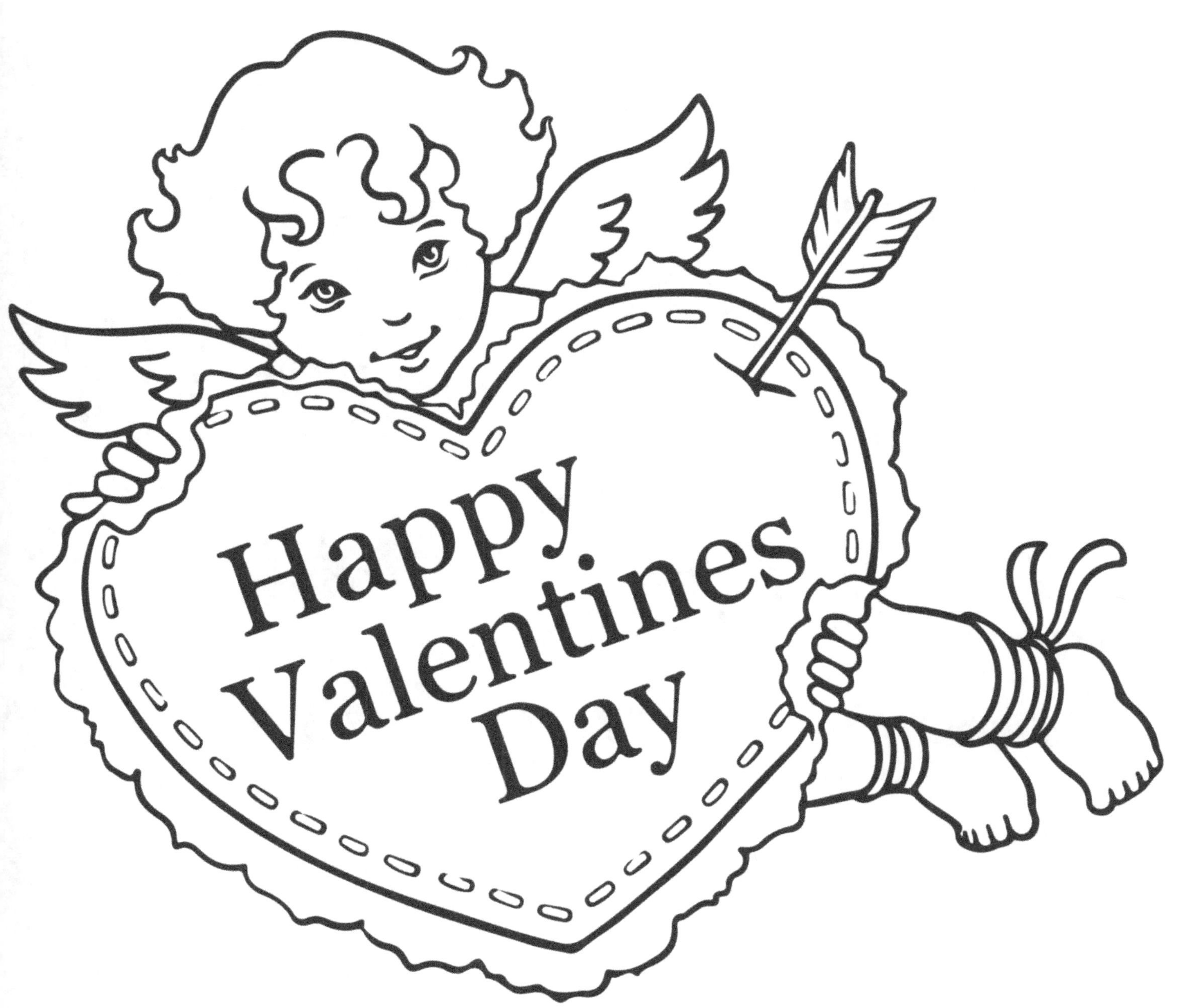

Happy
Valentines
Day

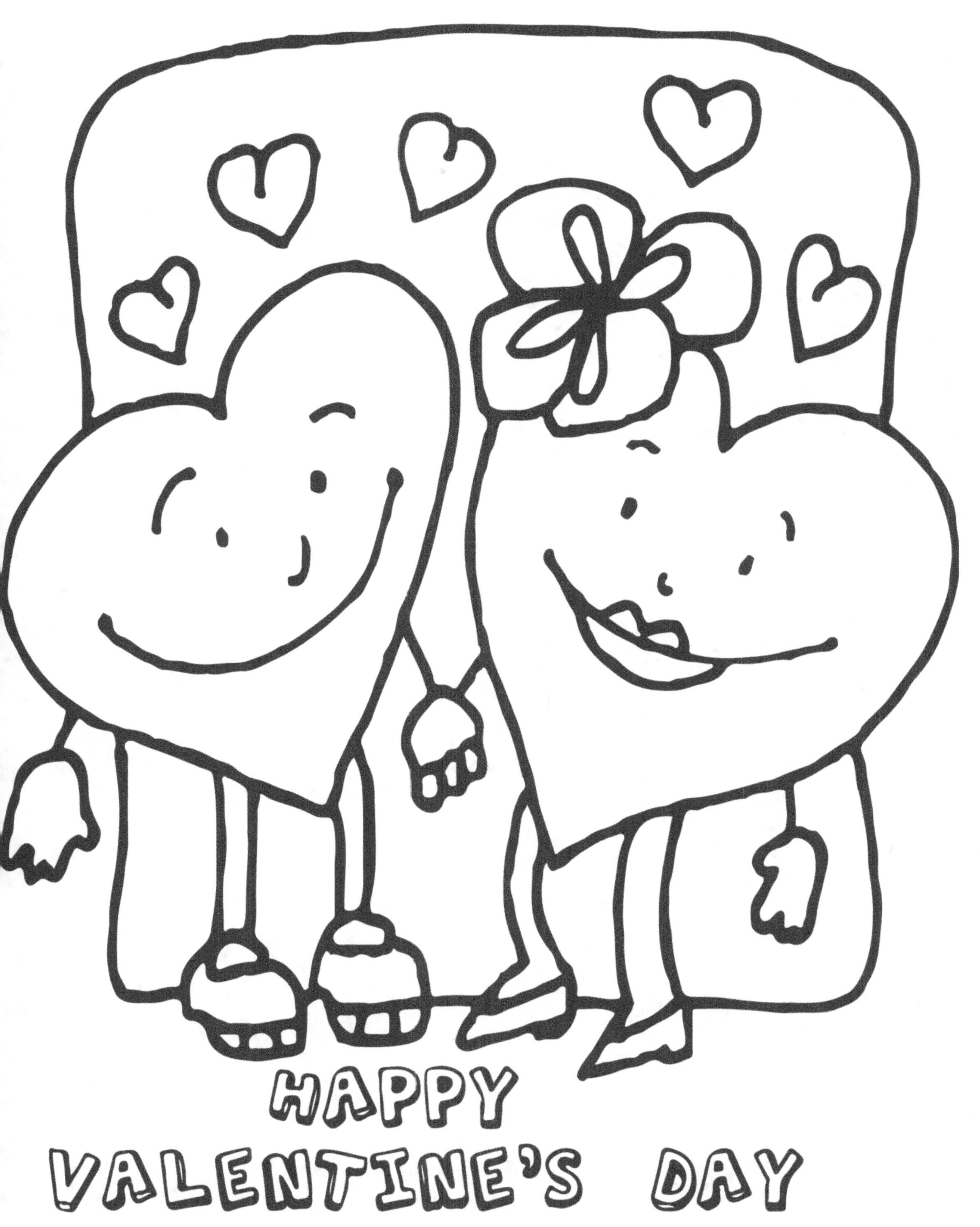

HAPPY
VALENTINE'S DAY

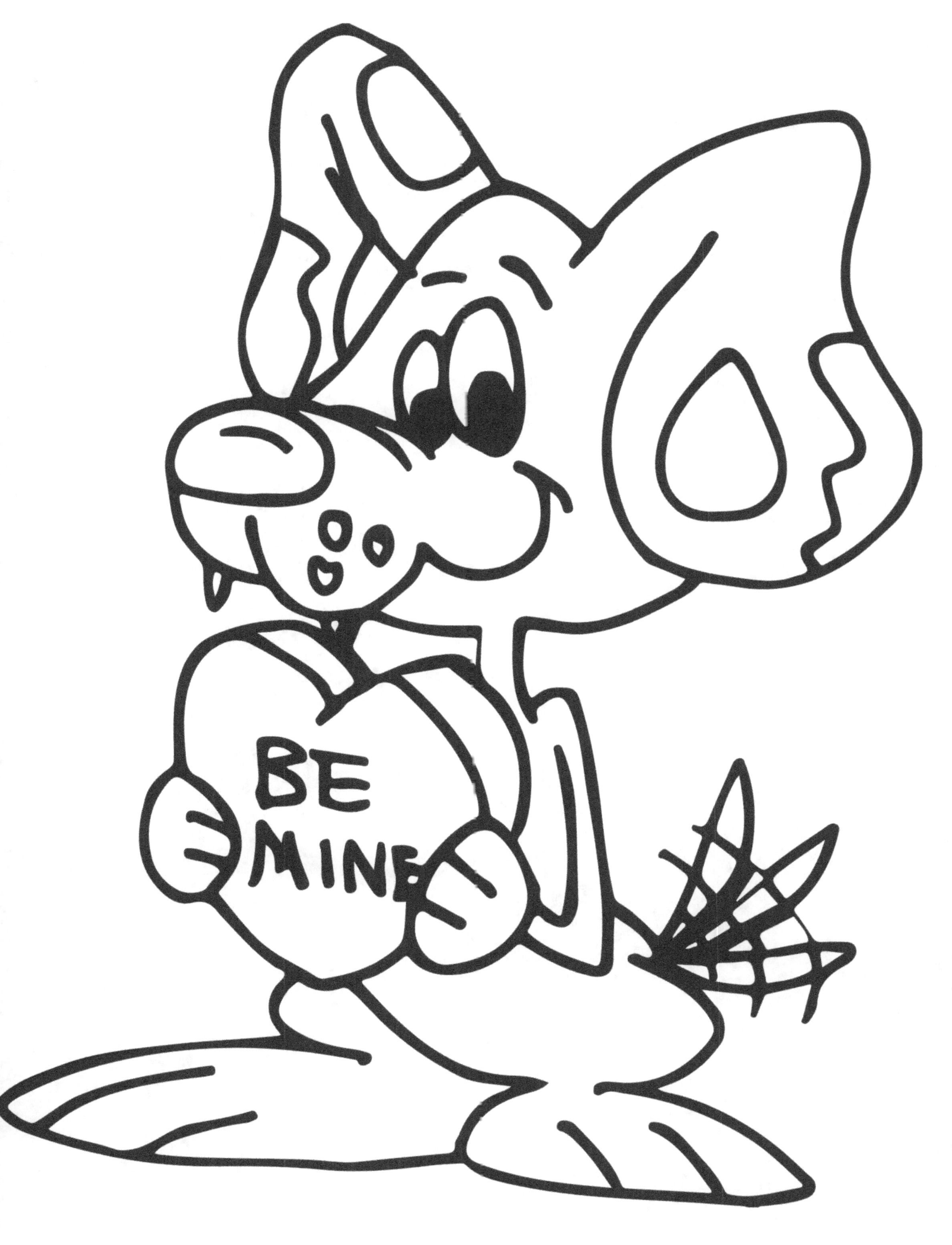
BE
MINE

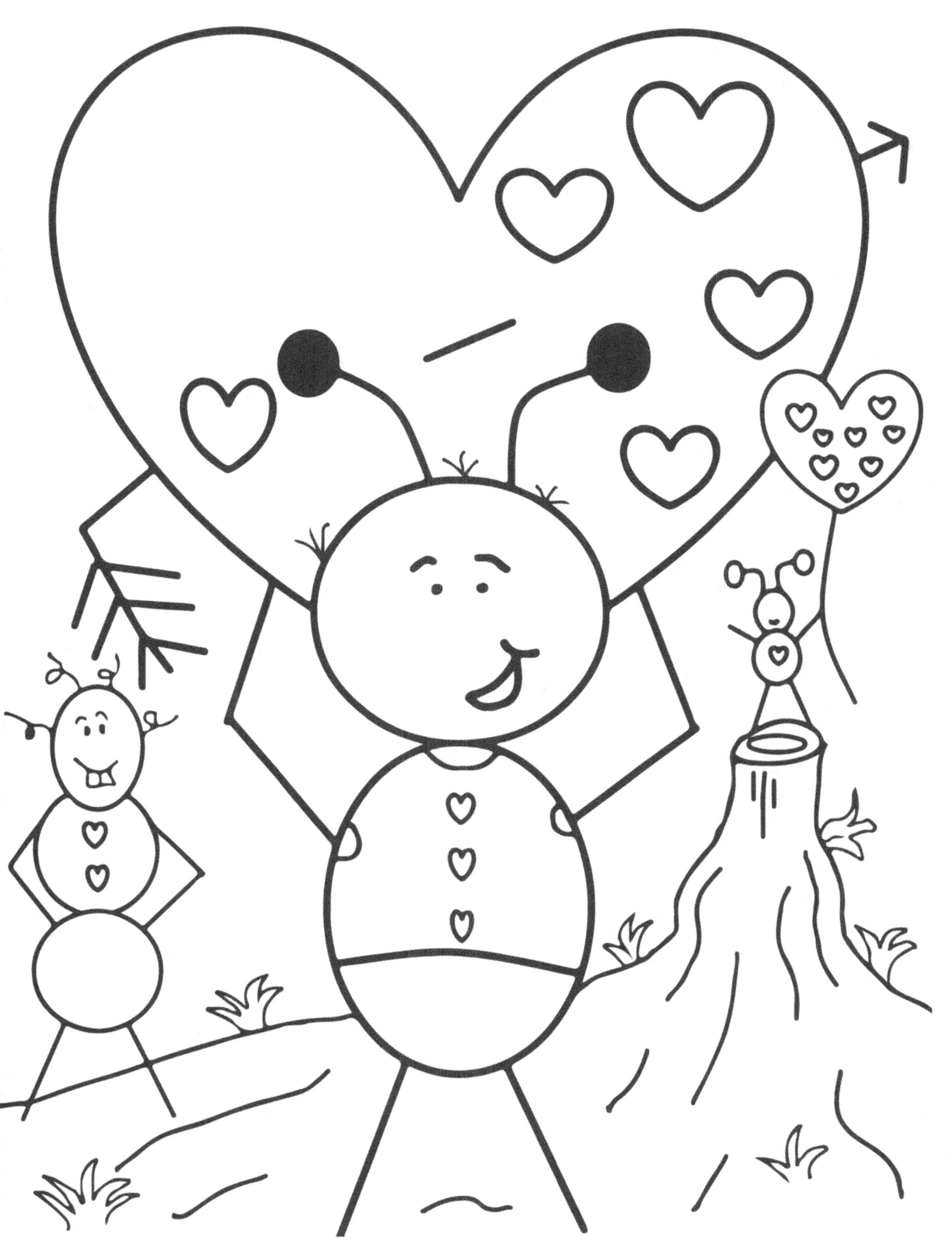

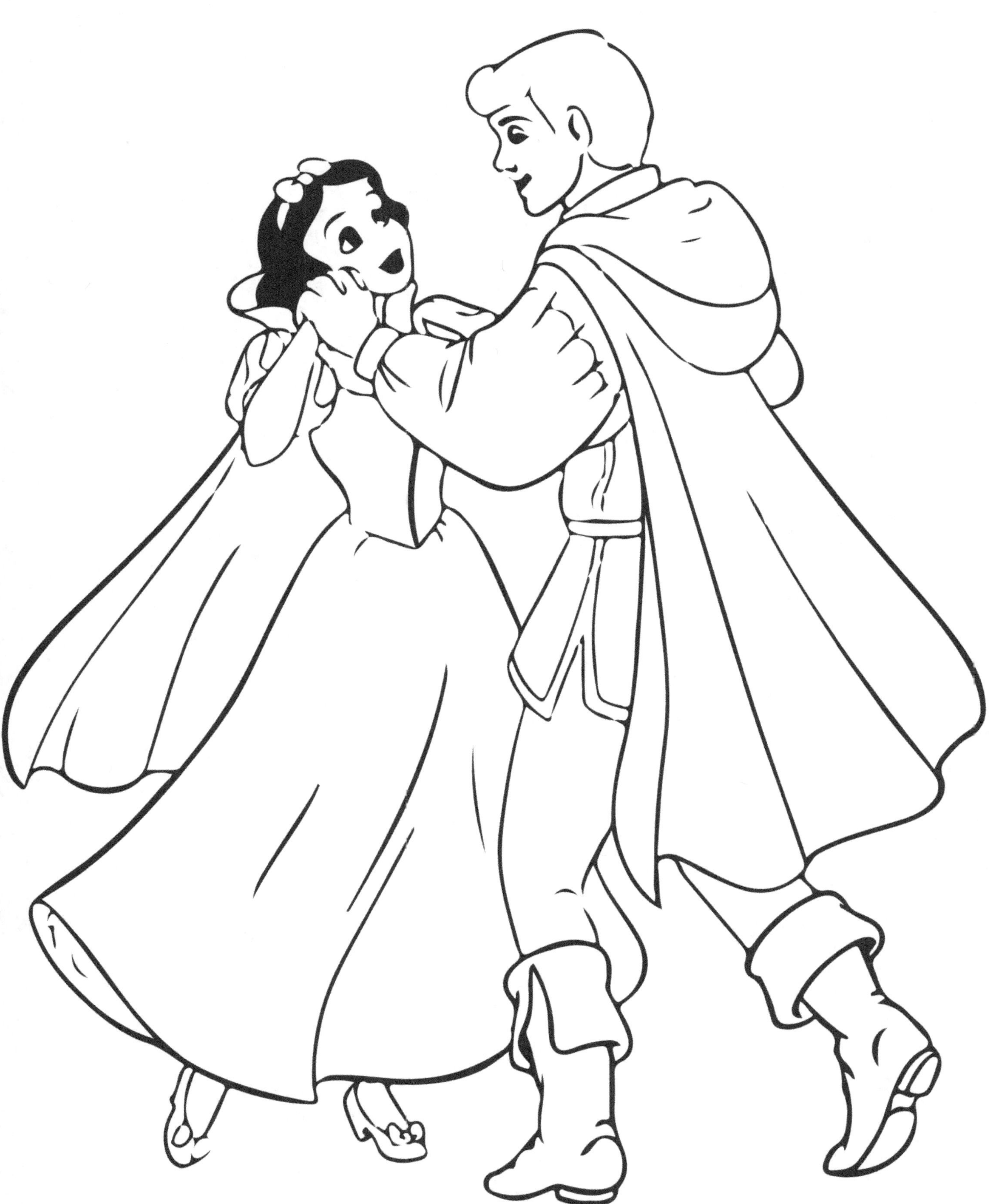

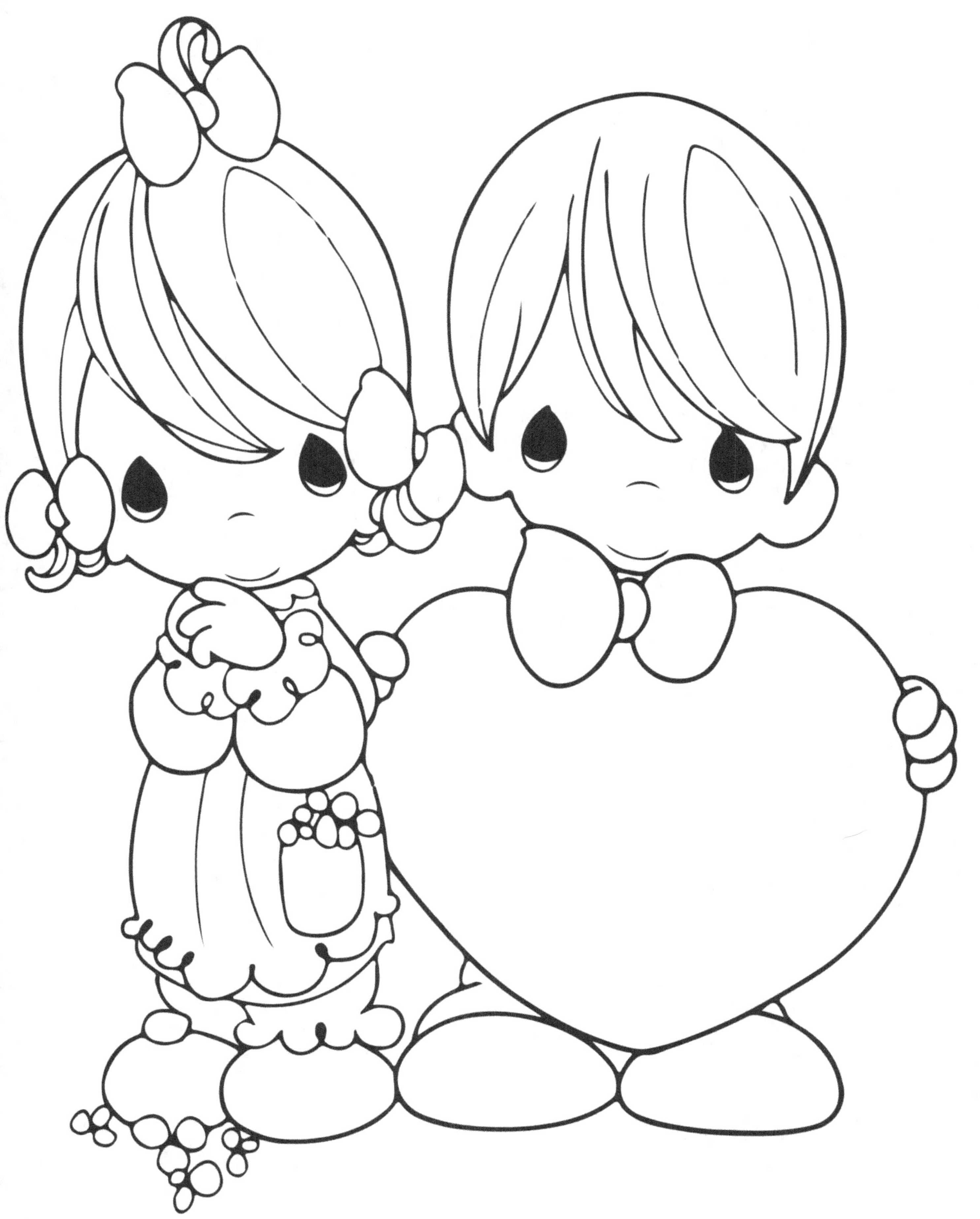

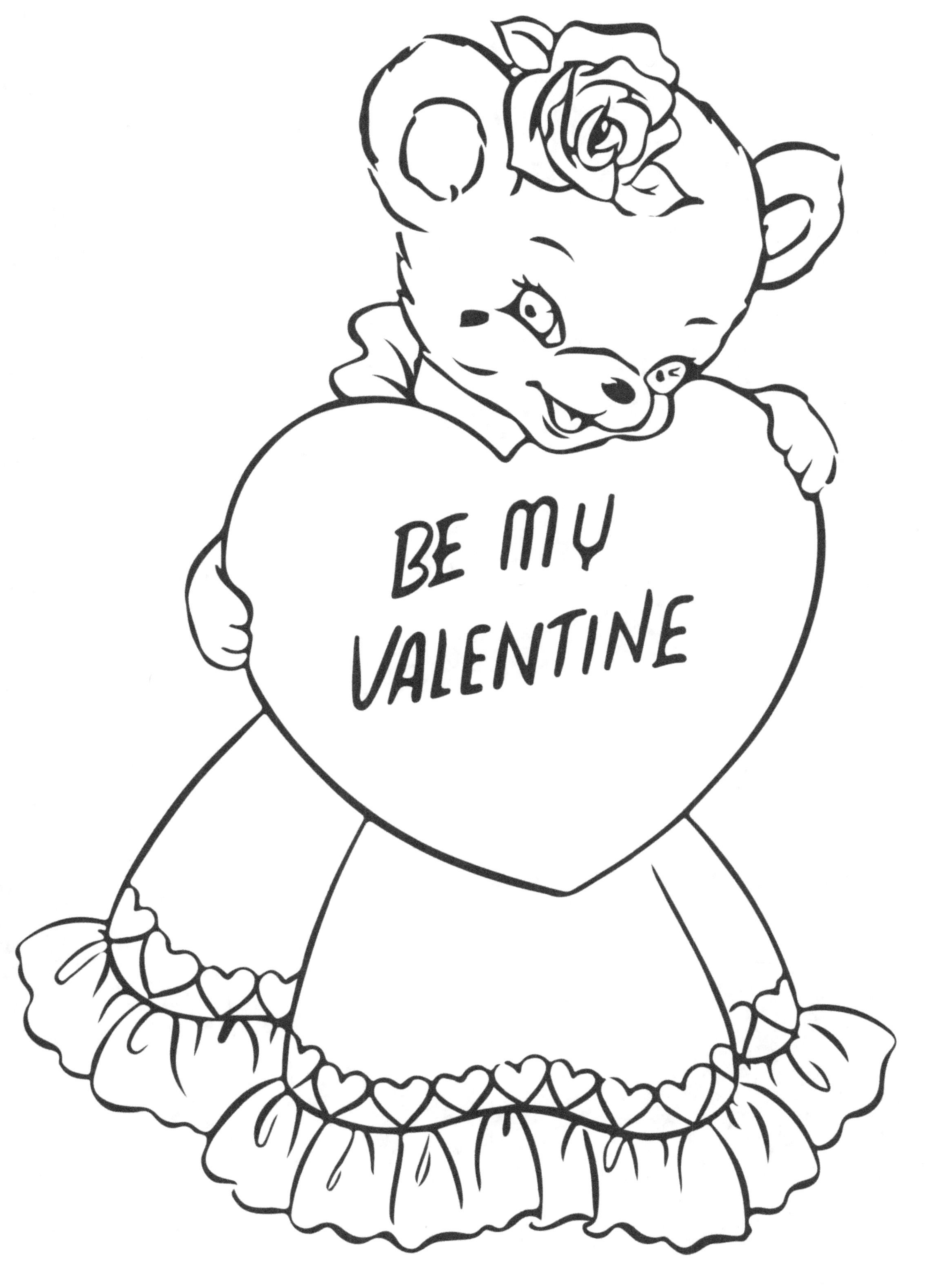
BE MY
VALENTINE

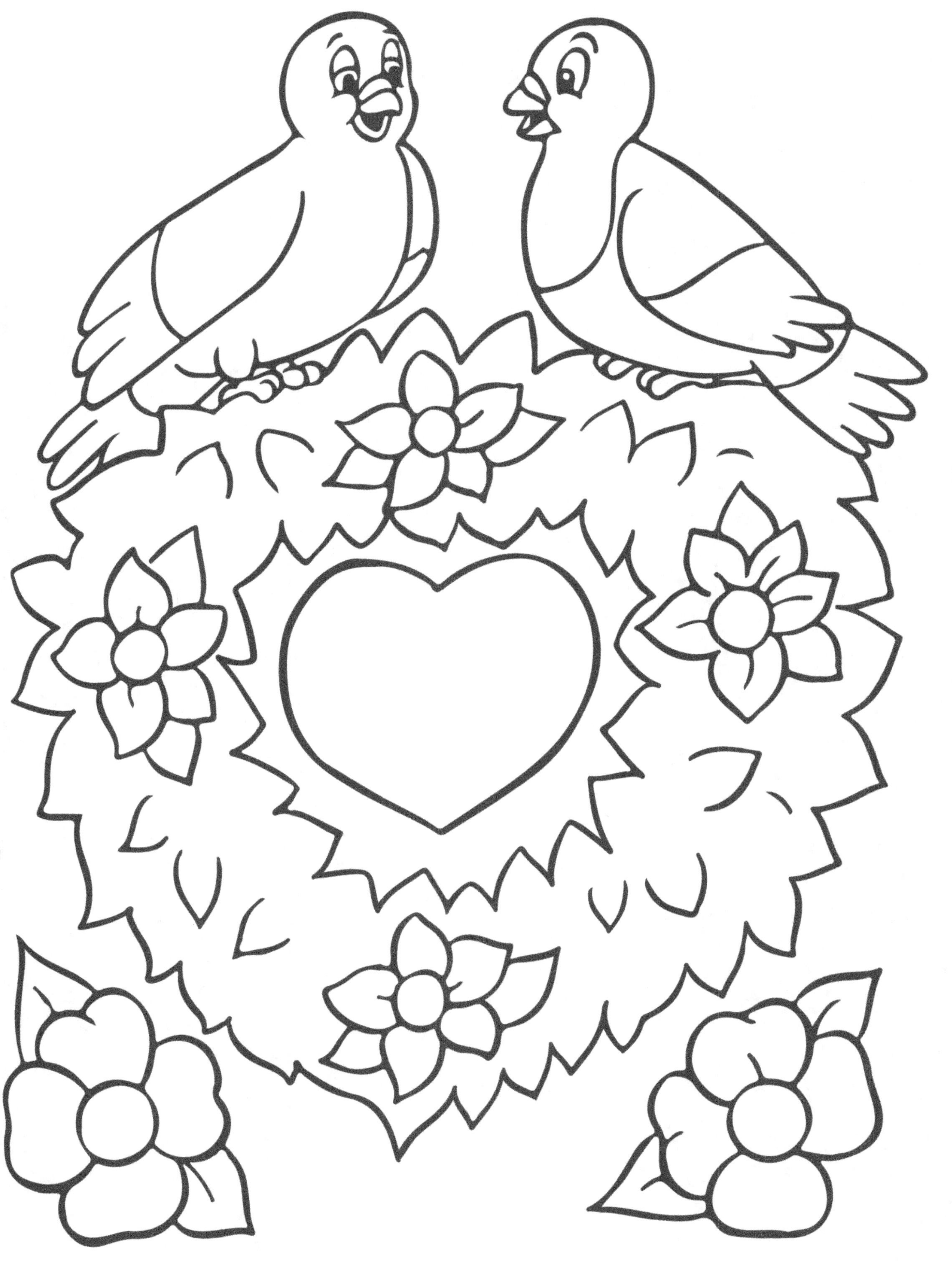

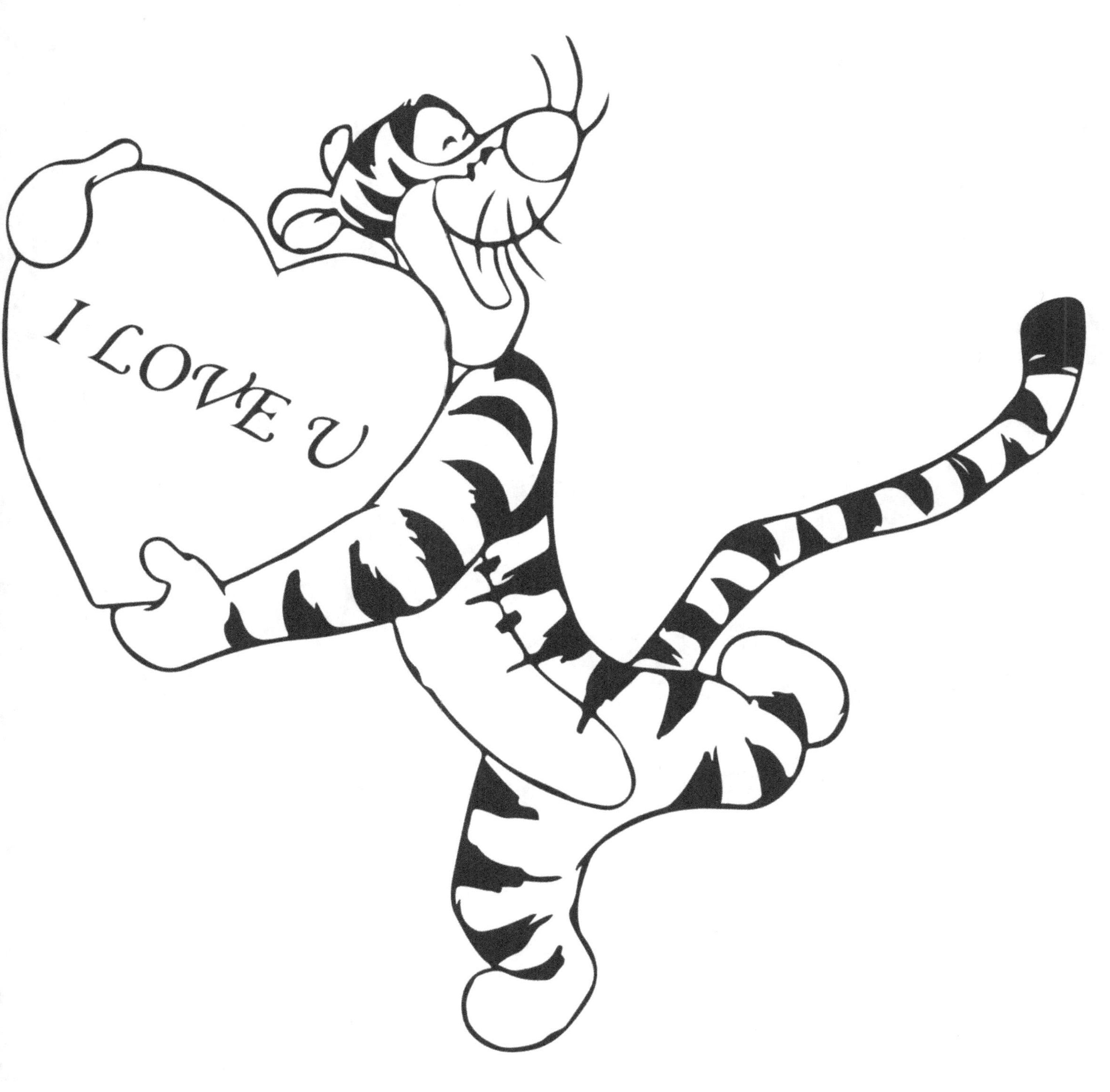

I LOVE U

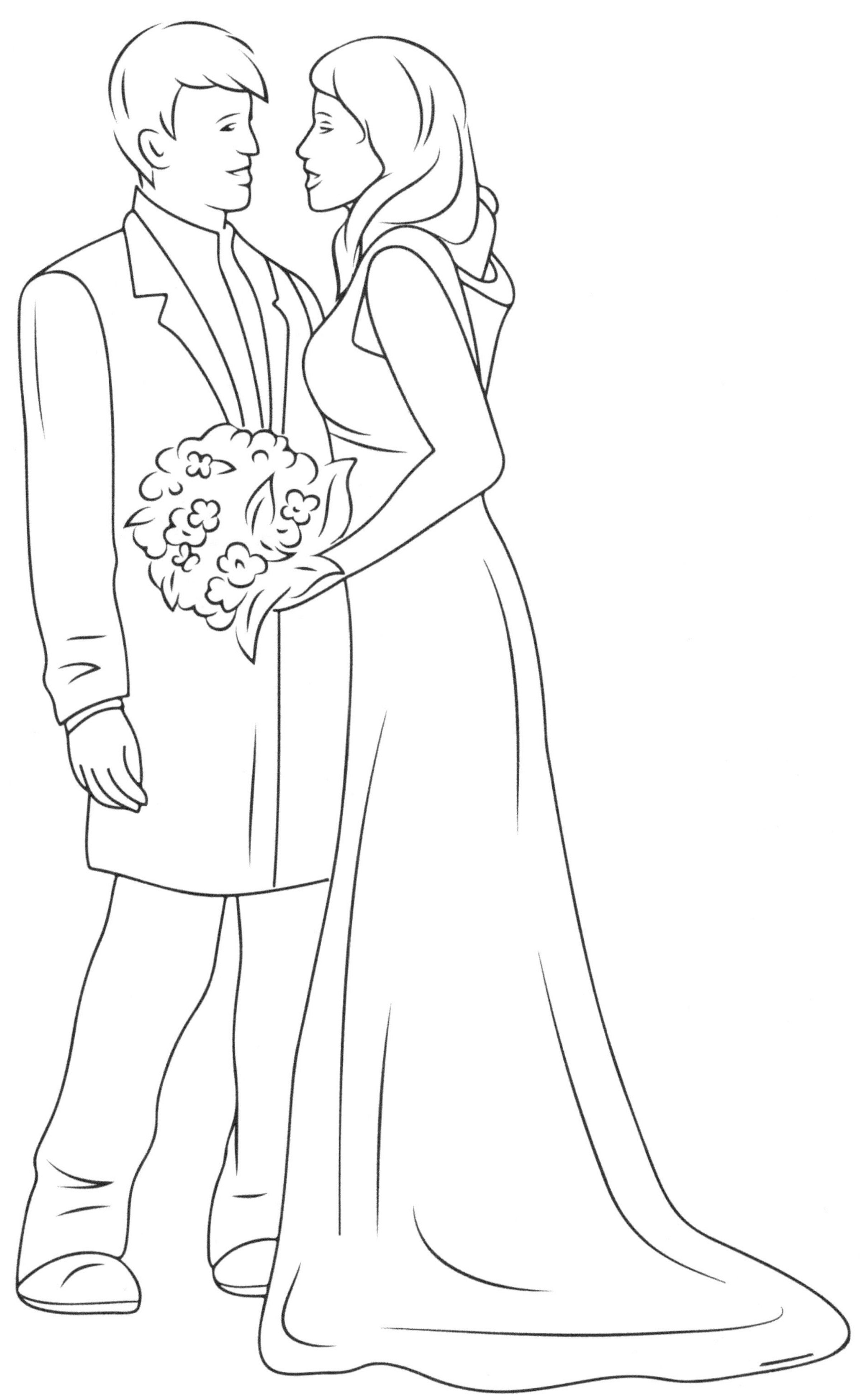

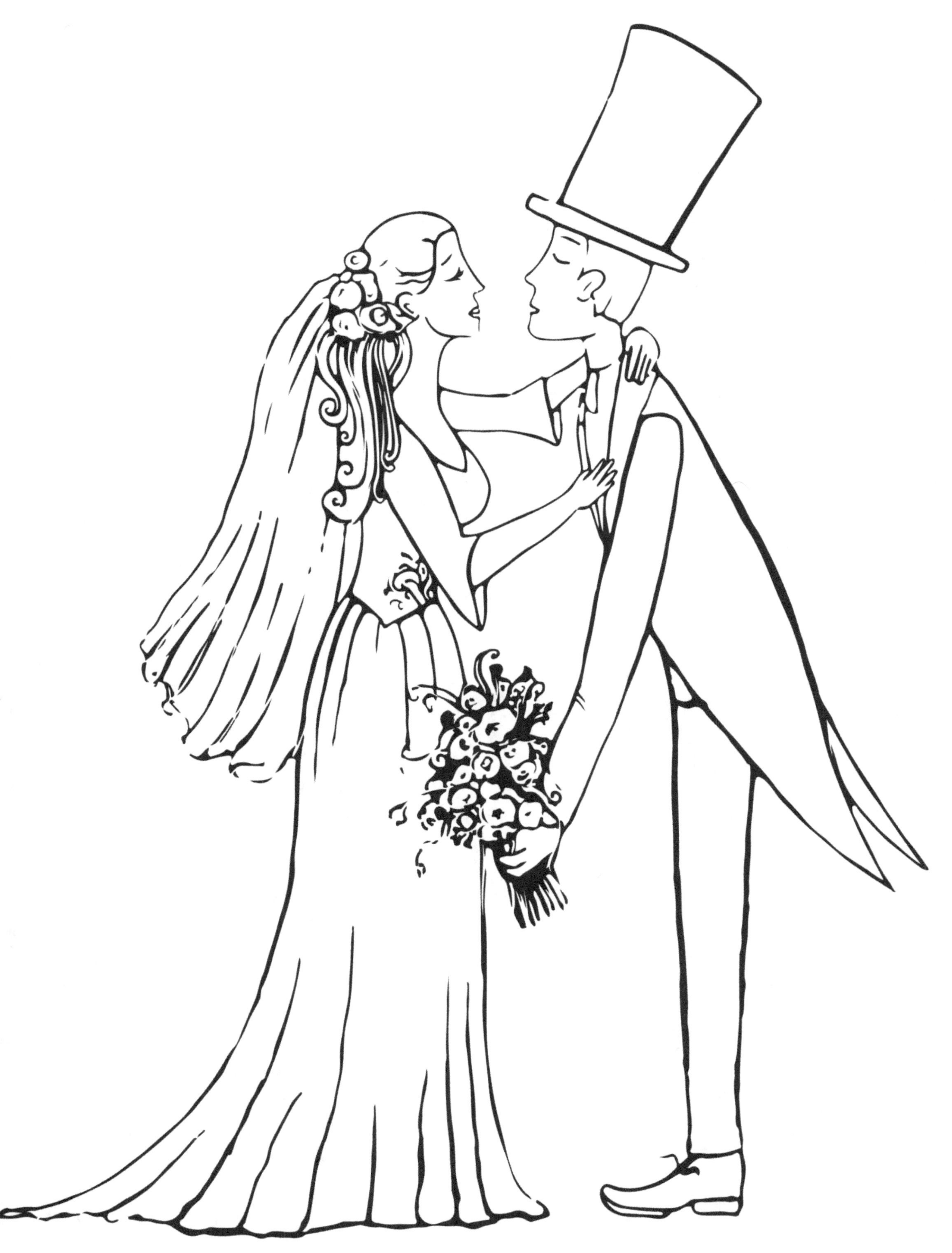

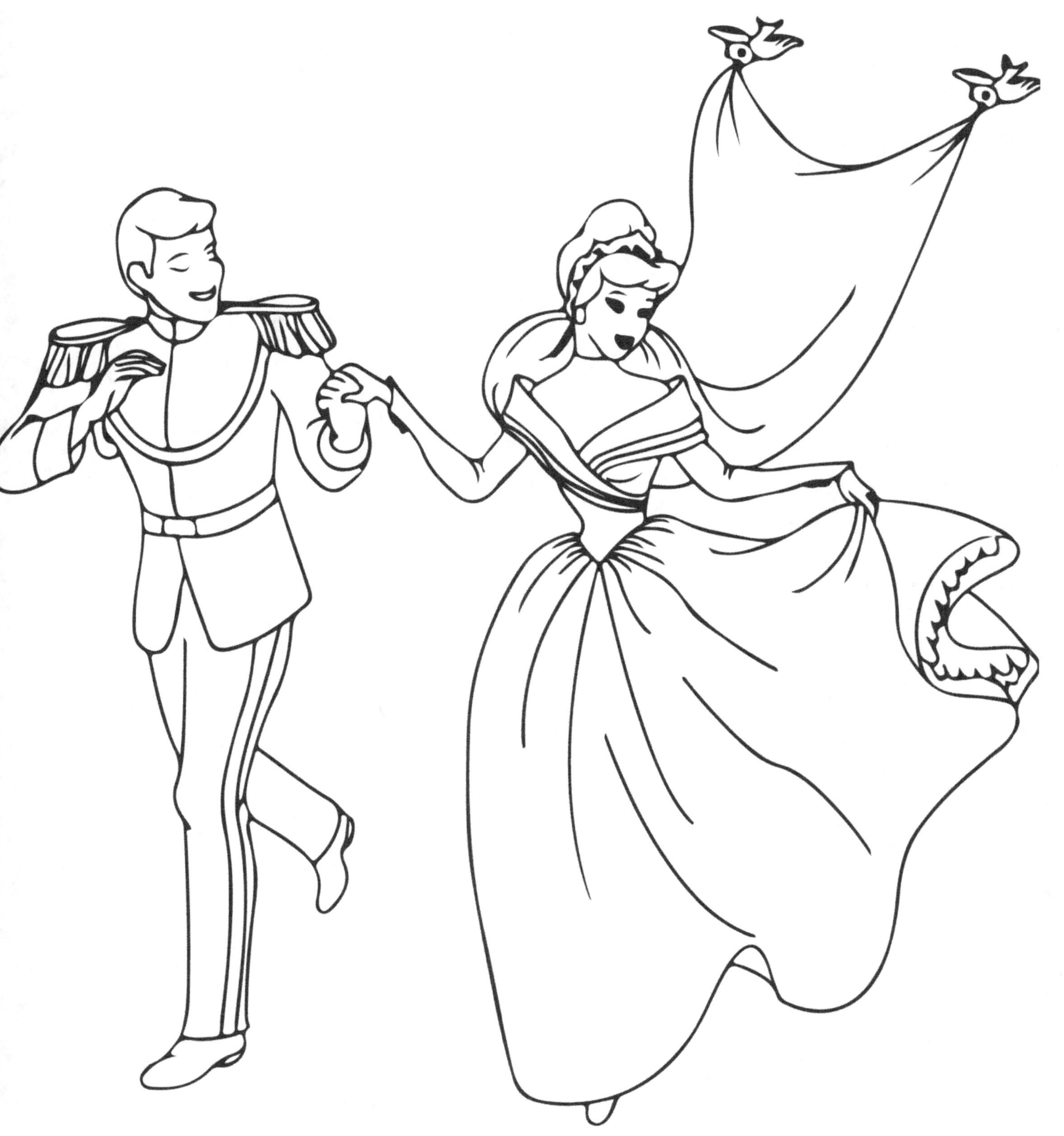

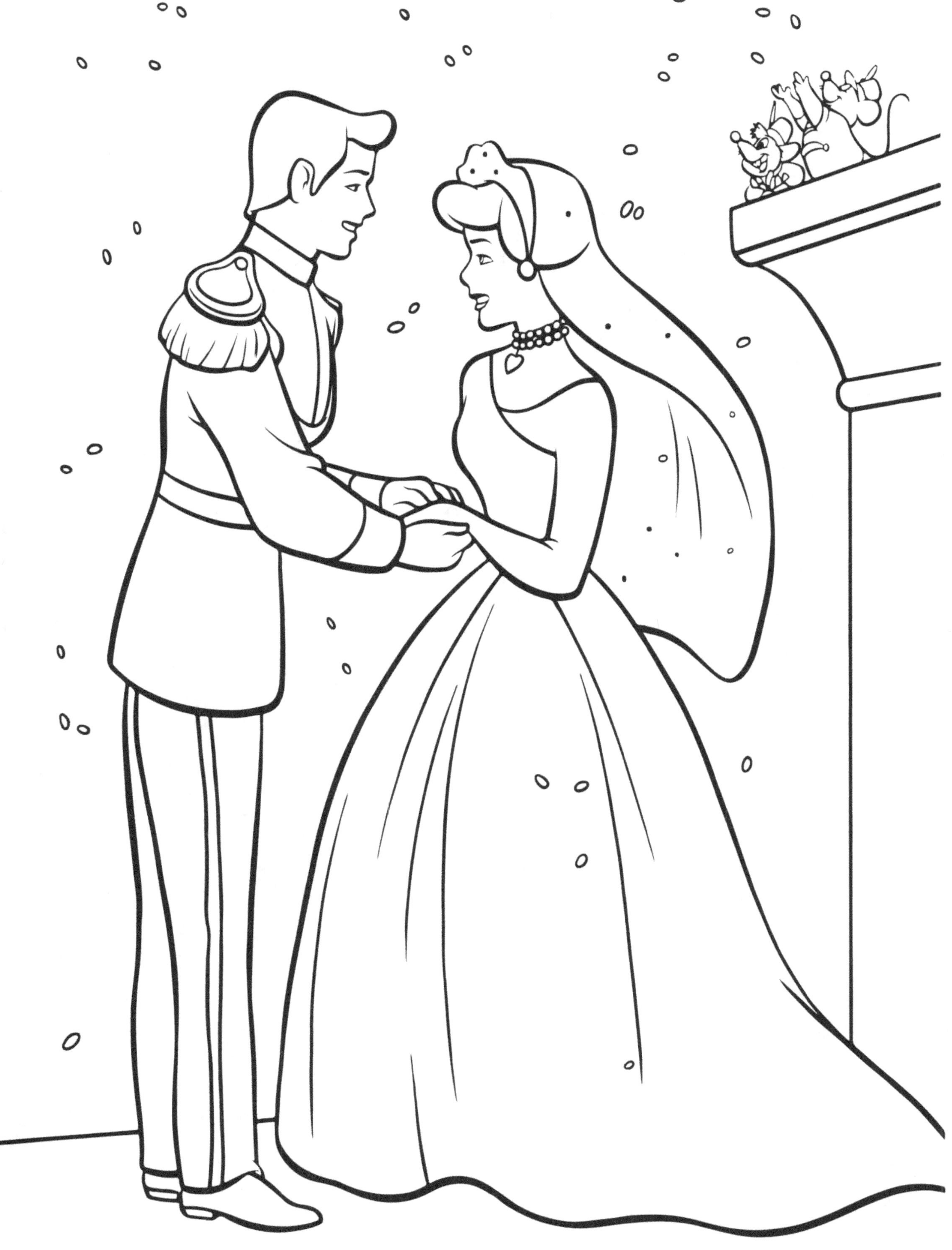

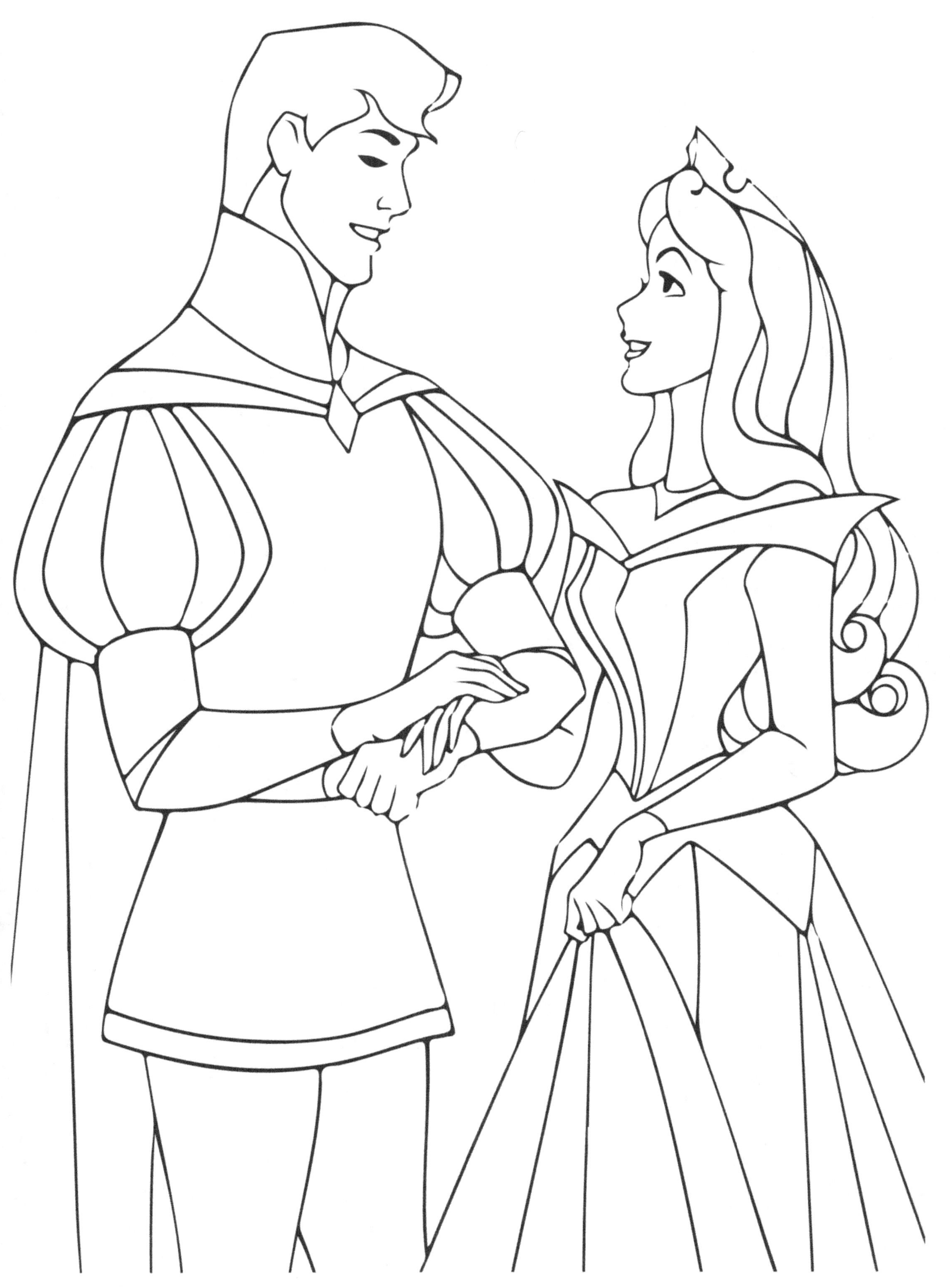

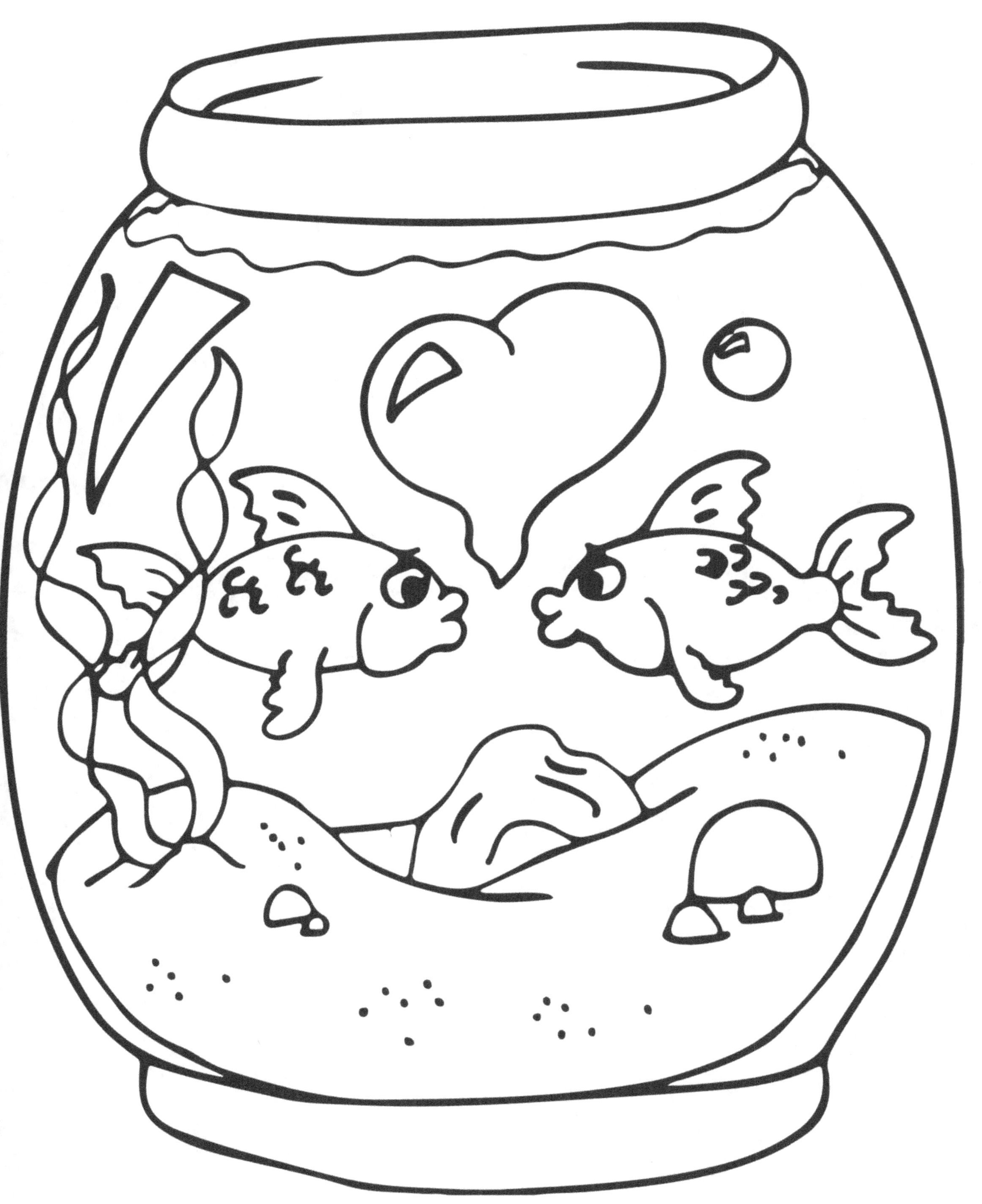

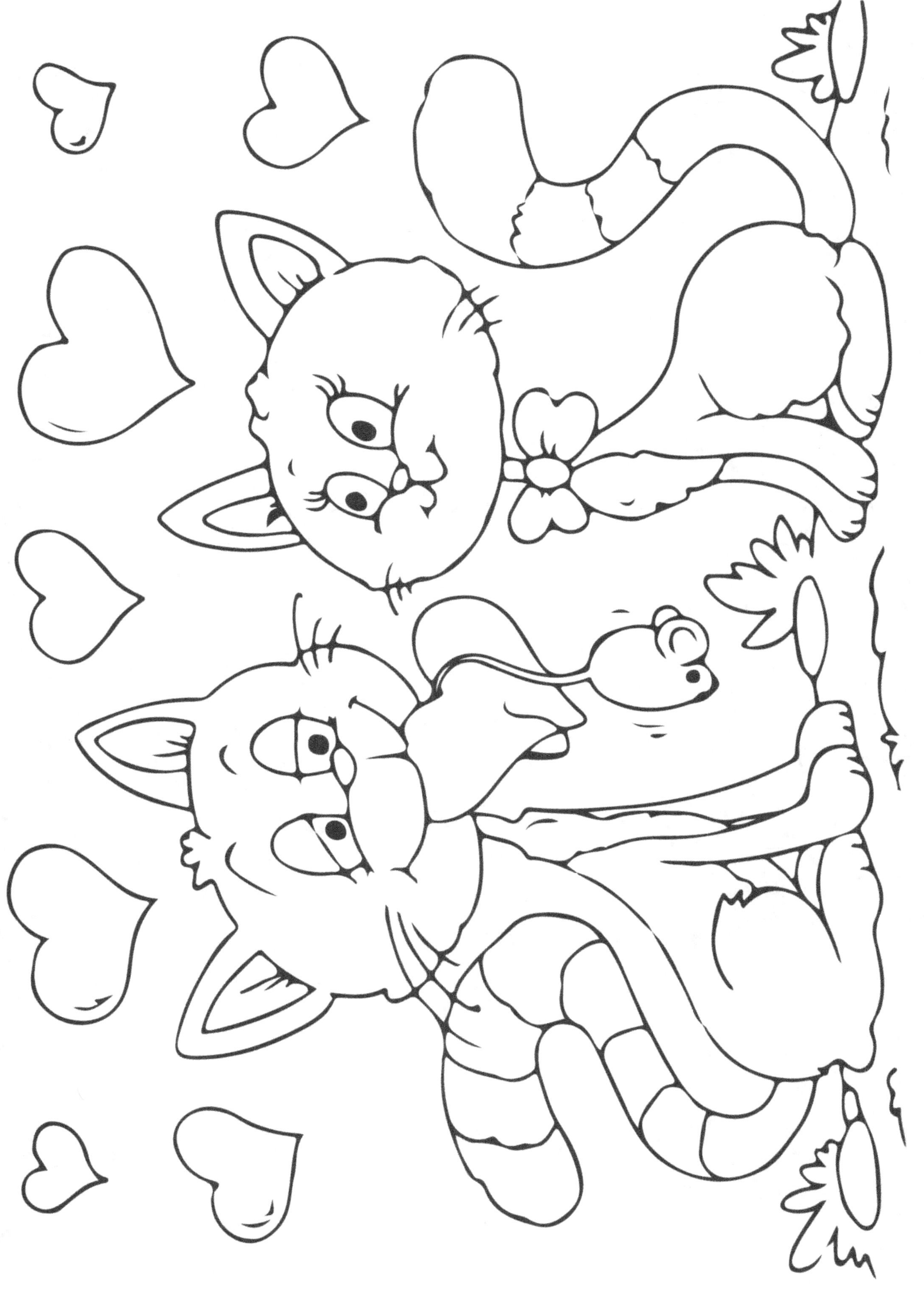

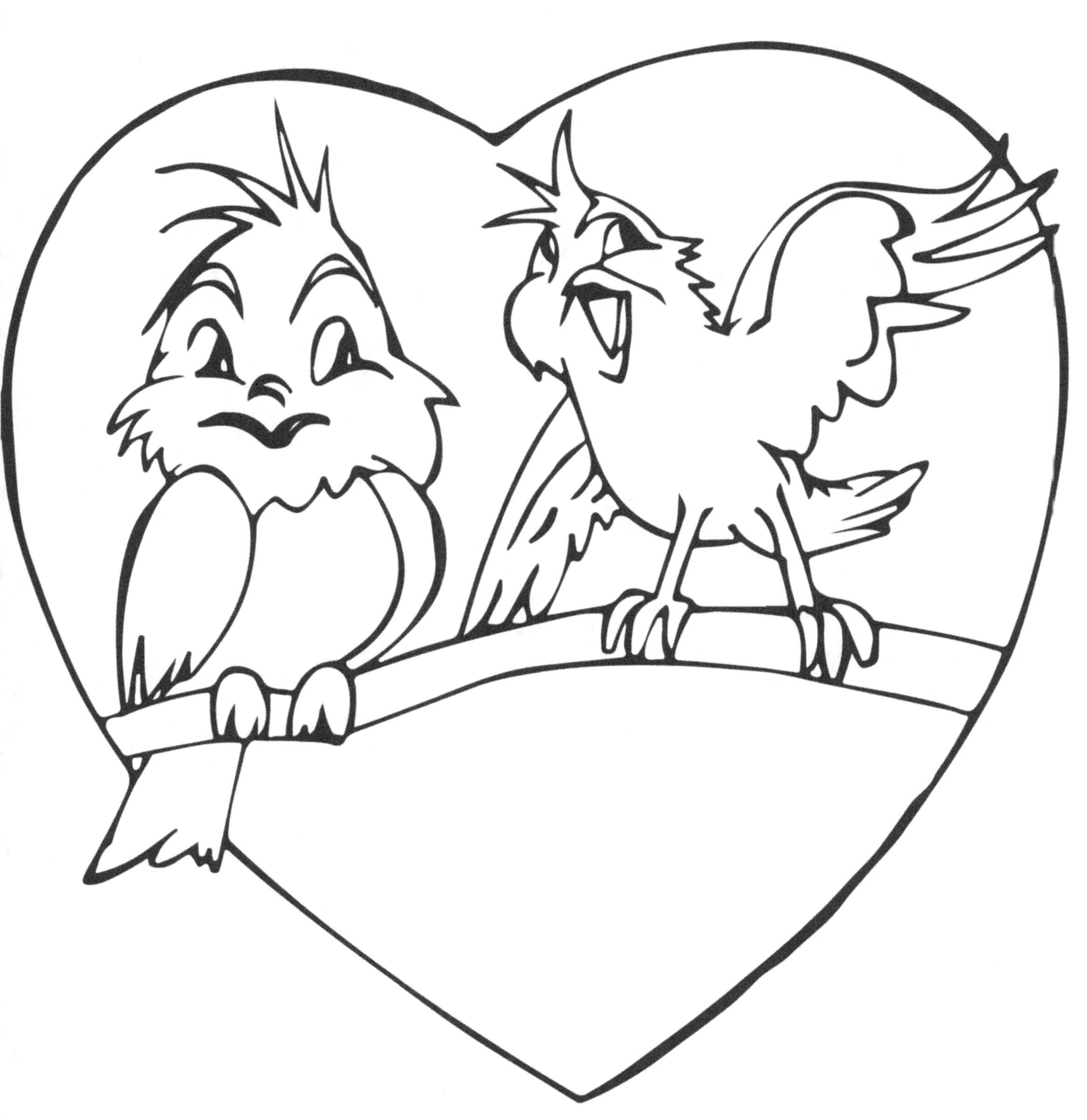

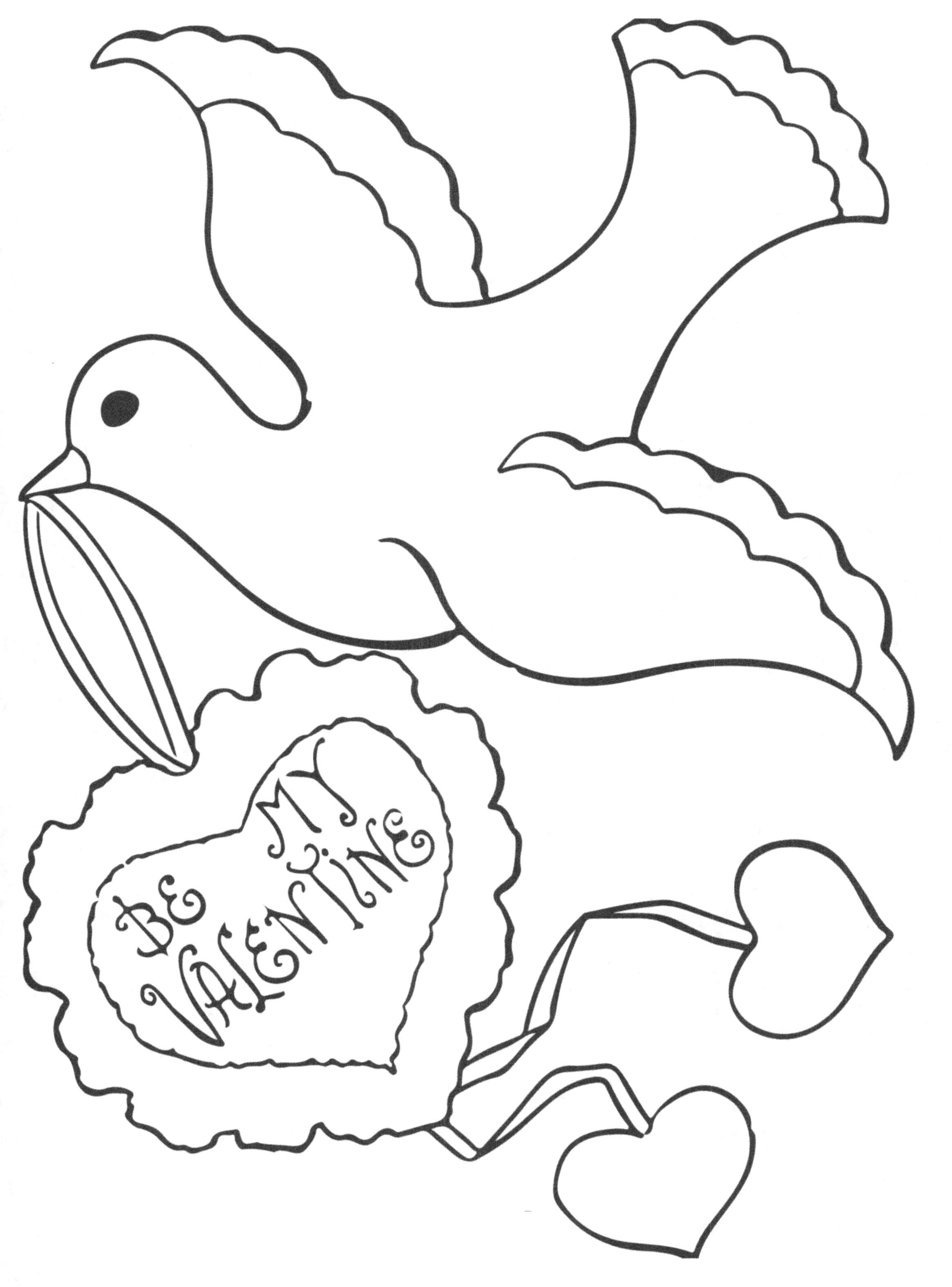

BE MY
VALENTINE

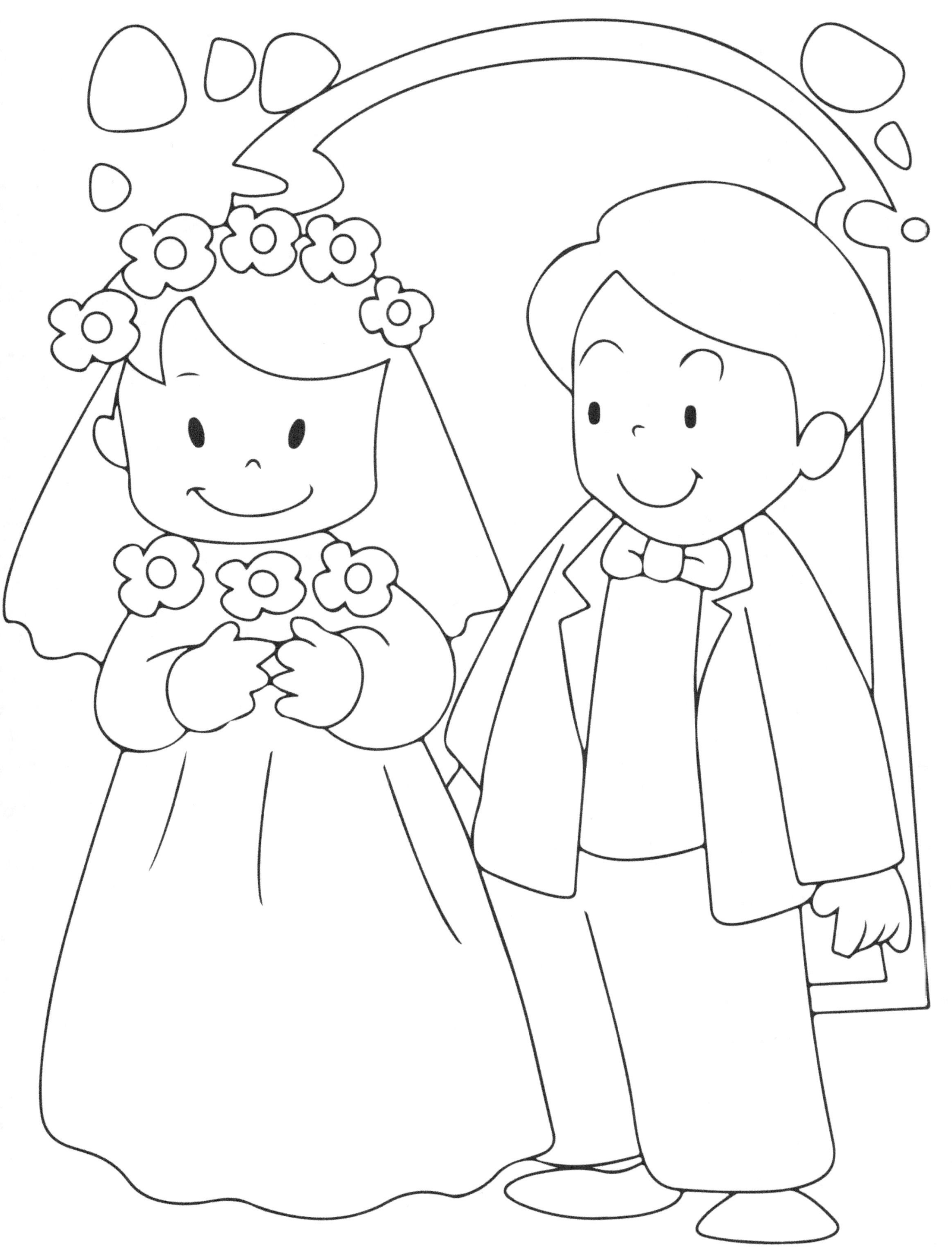

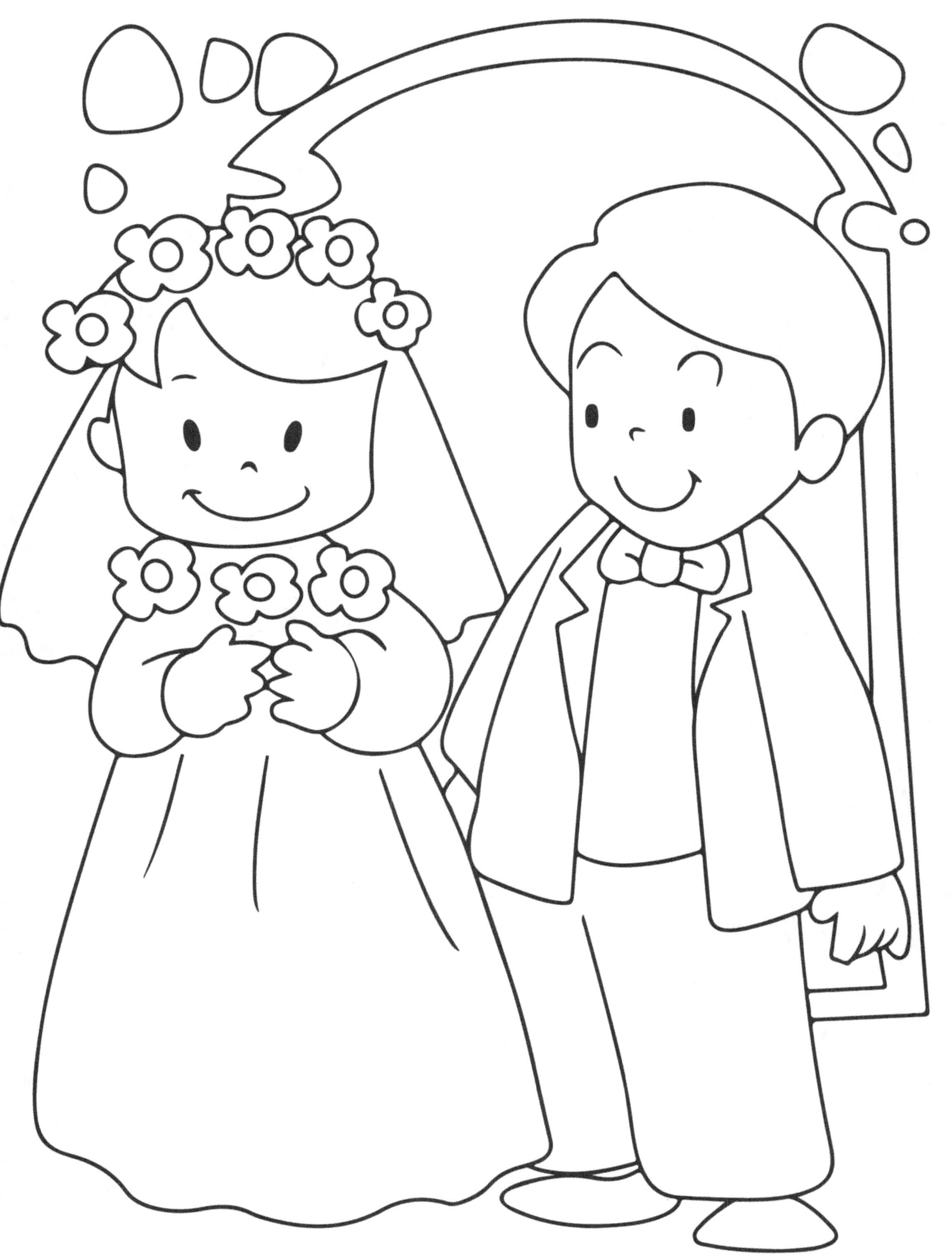

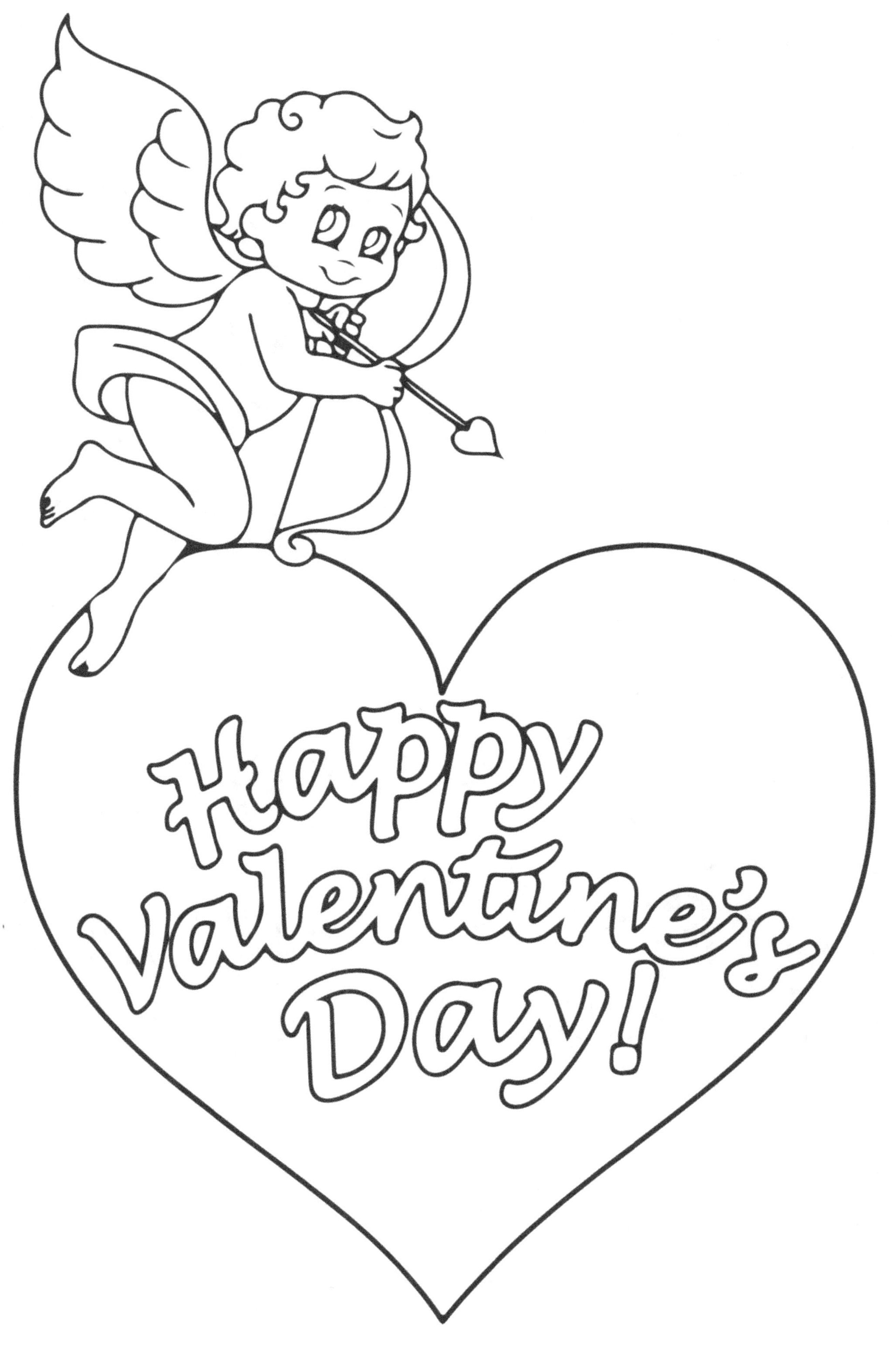

Happy
Valentine's
Day!

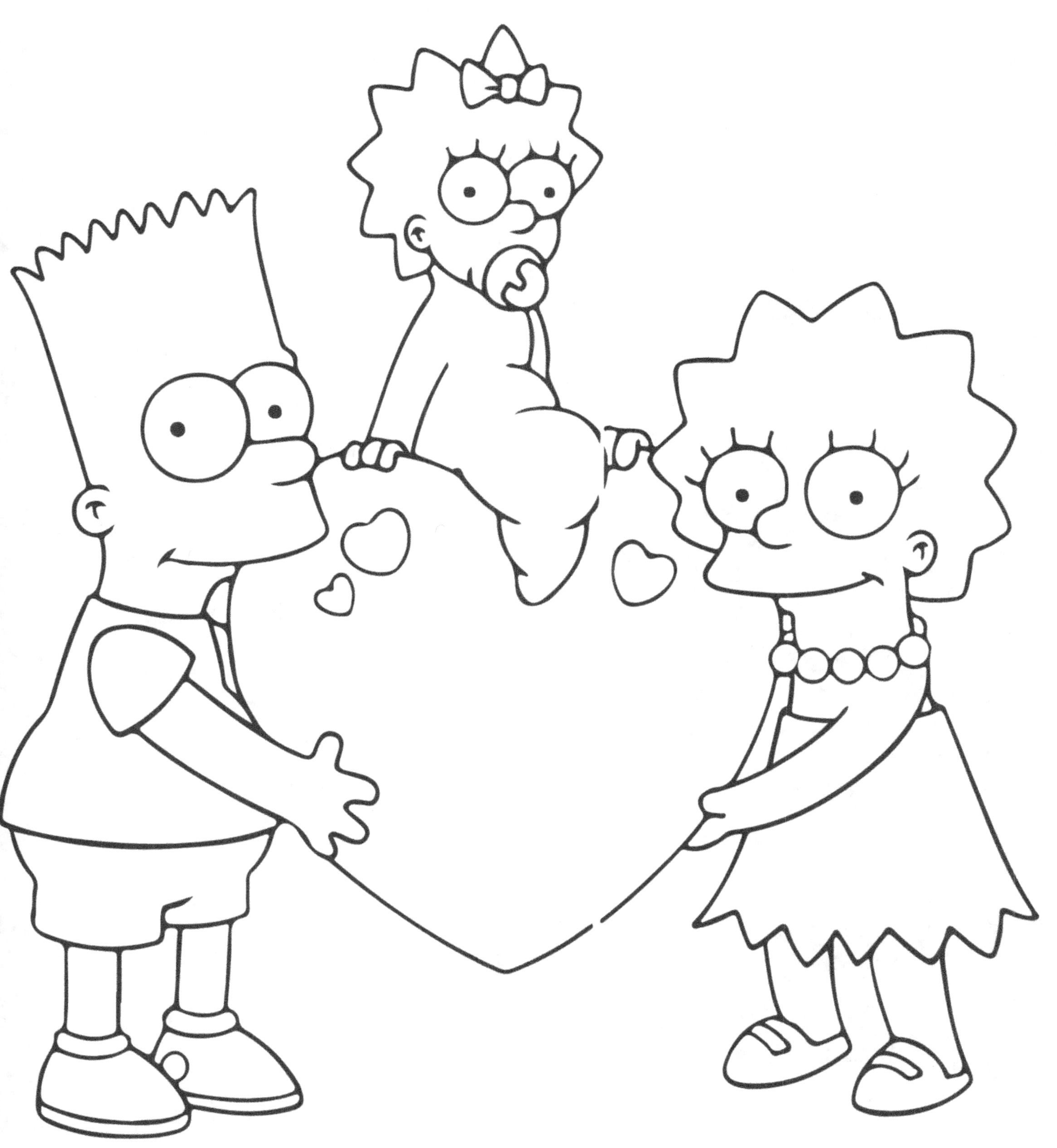

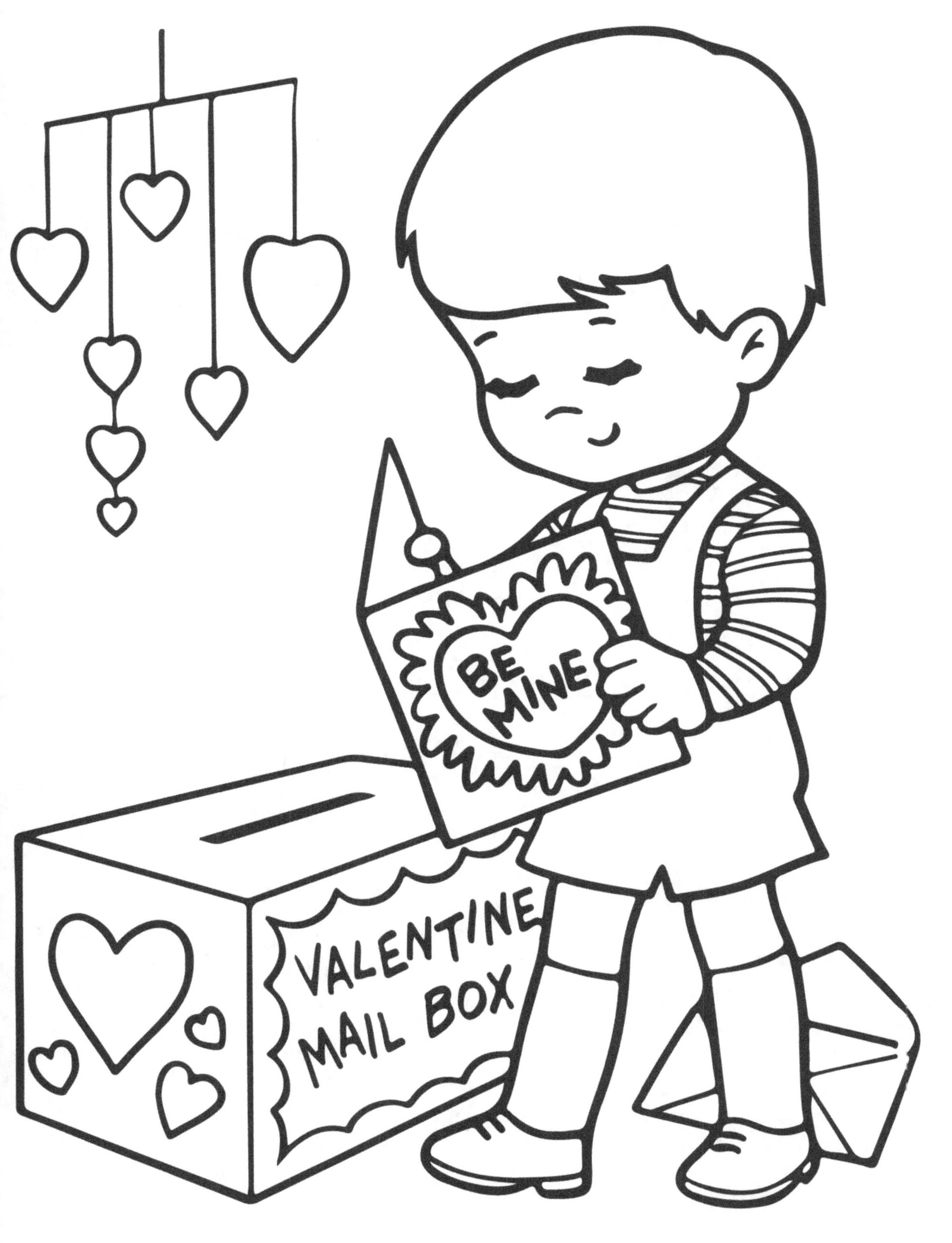

BE MINE
VALENTINE MAIL BOX